ABOUT THE MILKY WAY (OUR HOME GALAXY): 3RD GRADE SCIENCE TEXTBOOK SERIES

SPEEDY
PUBLISHING

Speedy Publishing LLC
40 E. Main St. #1156
Newark, DE 19711
www.speedypublishing.com

Copyright 2015

All Rights reserved. No part of this book may be reproduced or used in any way or form or by any means whether electronic or mechanical, this means that you cannot record or photocopy any material ideas or tips that are provided in this book

The Milky Way is one of many galaxies that lie in the universe. The Milky Way Galaxy is our home galaxy in the universe.

The Milky Way
began forming
around 12 billion
years ago. The
Milky Way is
part of cluster
of around 3,000
galaxies called
the Local Group.

The Milky Way is made up of at least 100 billion stars, as well as dust and gas. The center of the Milky Way contains a black hole that sucks up anything that crosses it.

The Milky Way is so named because across the night sky, it has a milky appearance.

The Milky Way
is very big and
takes about 200
million years
to make one
complete rotation.

The closest galaxy
to the Milky Way
is Andromeda,
which is around
2.6 million light
years away
from us.

It takes over two
hundred million
years for the sun
to orbit the center
of the galaxy.
This is called a
galactic year.

More than half
the stars found
in the Milky Way
are older than
the 4.5 billion
year old sun.

Made in the USA
Monee, IL
15 March 2020

23247117R00021